SELF

PRACTICE INSTRUCTIONS

Chapter One Quotes

by

Bhagavan Sri Ramana Maharshi
Sri Nisargadatta Maharaj
Sri Annamalai Swami
Sri Muruganar
Sri Sadhu Om
Sri Vasistha
Sri Sankara

Chapters Two, Three and Introduction

by

Anonymous Awareness

www.thefreedomreligionpress.com

www.seeseer.com

ISBN-13: 978-0-9797267-1-2

ISBN 10: 0-9797267-1-9

This book is sold with the understanding that the authors and publisher are not engaged in rendering psychological or medical advice. If expert assistance or counseling is required, the services of a licensed professional should be sought. The teachings and methods described in this book are of a religious or spiritual nature.

CONTENTS

INTRODUCTION

The most direct and rapid means to Self Realization goes by various names including:

A. *Self Inquiry.*
B. *Self Abidance.*
C. *Self Attention.*
D. *Self Awareness.*
E. *Abiding as Awareness.*
F. *Awareness of Awareness.*
G. *Awareness Aware of Itself.*
H. *Awareness Watching Awareness.*

In Chapter One the Seven Sages tell you about Self Awareness and how to practice it.

Chapter Two has step by step practice instructions for the Awareness Watching Awareness Method. It begins with the preliminary instructions and following that are the Practice Instructions.

Chapter Three further clarifies how to practice the Awareness Watching Awareness Method.

The purpose of the Self Awareness Practice is to bring the impostor self to its final end so that you can remain eternally as your true Self which is Absolutely Perfect Infinite-Awareness-Love-Bliss that has never experienced any sorrow or suffering in all of eternity.

The impostor self is very deceptive and has millions of potential strategies to preserve its imaginary self. There are as many such strategies as there are possible combinations of thoughts, ideas, beliefs, concepts and opinions. The Two Great Keys to stop the impostor self from using those strategies are:

*1.	The awakening of the extremely intense desire for Liberation.*

*2.	Self honesty. Self honesty begins by actually seeing the impostor self's preservation strategies.*

The quotes in Chapter One are the same as the quotes in Chapter (Step) Seven from the book The Seven Steps to Awakening. Chapters Two and Three are essentially the same as Chapters Seven and Eight from the book The Most Direct Means to Eternal Bliss.

Self Awareness Practice Instructions is Book One in a series of six books called the Self Realization Series. One purpose of the Self Realization Series is to put just one category of quotes into a small book that has the advantage of making it easier to focus, meditate on, grasp, and have insight into just one subject at a time. That makes the approach simple, easier and less complicated.

The idea is to stay focused on just one subject until you have received everything you need to receive from that one subject.

Most people go on to the next subject without ever having learned to apply to their lives the subject they are studying now.

The Self Realization series of books are practice manuals aimed at helping sincere seekers of Self Realization master one Key to Self Realization at a time.

CHAPTER ONE

SELF AWARENESS

PRACTICE INSTRUCTIONS

BHAGAVAN SRI RAMANA MAHARSHI
(1439 – 1450)

1439.　　If you observe awareness steadily,
this awareness itself as Guru
will reveal the Truth.

1440.　　Instead of looking outward
at objects, you observe that looking.

1441.　　The only true and full awareness is
awareness of awareness.
Till awareness is awareness of itself,
it knows no peace at all.

1442.　　True natural awareness which goes
not after alien objects is the Heart.
Since actionless awareness shines as real Being,
its joy consists in concentration on itself.

1443.   Not like other things unreal, but always by its Being real, the Self as permanent Awareness has no other dwelling place than its own radiant Awareness.

1444.   The Self, our Being, is Awareness.

1445.   The method of Self-inquiry is to turn the outward going mind back to its source, the Heart, the Self, and fix it ever there, preventing the rising of the empty "I."

1446.   Inquiry is making the mind abide firm in the Self till the false ego, illusion's seed, has perished.

1447.   One who has wisely chosen the straight path of Self-inquiry can never go astray; for like the bright, clear Sun, the Self reveals itself direct to whoso turns towards it.

1448.   Undeluded by whatever else may come and go, unwinking watch the Self, because the little fault of forgetting for one moment one's true Being as Pure Awareness brings tremendous loss.

1449.   If you refrain from looking
at this or that
or any other object
then by that overpowering look
into absolute Being
you become yourself
the boundless space
of pure Awareness
which alone is real Being.

1450.   Unbroken Self-awareness
is the true, bright path
of devotion or love.

Knowledge of our inherent nature
as indivisible Bliss supreme
wells up as love.

SRI ANNAMALAI SWAMI
(1451 – 1458)

1451.   Questioner: But is it enough to be aware of the awareness?

Annamalai Swami: You are repeating the question, so I will repeat the answer.

If you remain in the state of consciousness, there will be nothing apart from it.

No problems, no misery, no questions.

1452.   Ignorance is ignorance of the Self, and to remove it Self-awareness is required. When you come to an awareness of the Self, ignorance vanishes. If you don't lose contact with the Self, ignorance can never arise.

1453.   Bhagavan spoke about turning inwards to face the Self. That is all that is needed. If we look outwards, we become entangled with objects and we lose awareness of the Self shining within us. But when, by repeated practice, we gain the strength to keep our focus on the Self within, we become one with it and the darkness of self-ignorance vanishes.

1454.   Tayumanuvar,
a Tamil saint whom Bhagavan often quoted,
wrote in one of his poems:

> "My Guru merely told me that
> I am consciousness.

Having heard this, I held unto consciousness. What he told me was just one sentence, but I cannot describe the bliss I attained from holding onto that one simple sentence. Through that one sentence I attained a peace and a happiness that can never be explained in words."

1455.   You can only put your attention on one thing at a time. While it is on the mind or the body, it cannot be on the Self. Conversely, if you put attention on the Self and become absorbed in it, there will be no awareness of mind and body.

1456.   You have forcibly to drag
your wandering attention back to the Self
each time it shows an interest
in going anywhere else.

1457.   While the search was on,
that which was being sought was,
in reality, that through which the seeing
was taking place.

You were looking for an object
that finally turned out to be
the subject that was doing the seeing.

1458.   Even the sequence,
"To whom has this thought come? To me,"
is based on ignorance of the truth.   Why?
Because it is verbalizing a state of ignorance;
it is perpetuating an erroneous assumption that
there is a person who is having troublesome
thoughts.

You are the Self,
not some make-believe person
who is having thoughts.

SRI SADHU OM
(1459 – 1465)

1459.   Clinging to the consciousness 'I' and thereby acquiring a greater and greater intensity of concentration upon it, is diving deep within. Instead of thus diving within, many, thinking that they are engaged in Self-inquiry, sit down for hours together simply repeating mentally or vocally, "Who am I?" or "Whence am I?." There are others again who, when they sit for inquiry, face their thoughts and endlessly repeat mentally the following questions taught by Sri Bhagavan: "To whom come these thoughts? To me; who am I?", or sometimes they even wait for the next thought to come up so that they can fling these questions at it! Even this is futile.

1460.   We should not remain watching "What is the next thought?"

Merely to keep on questioning in this manner is not Self-attention.

1461.   By saying,
"This is the direct path for all",
Sri Bhagavan points out that anyone,
however weak his mind may be,
can acquire through this path
that true strength of mind
which is required to abide in one's source.

Therefore, taking to Self-attention,
which is the real introversion,
is by itself far better
than giving any other target to the mind.

1462.   If our attention is directed
          only towards ourself,
          our knowledge of our existence
          alone is nourished,
          and since the mind is not attended to,
          it is deprived of its strength.

1463.   When,
through the aforesaid Self-attention,
we are more and more firmly fixed
in our existence-consciousness,
the tendencies will be destroyed
because there is no one to attend to them.

1464.　　The feeling 'I am'
　　　　　is the experience
　　　　　common to one and all.

1465.　　The pure existence-consciousness,
　　　　　'I am',
　　　　　is not a thought;
　　　　　this consciousness is our nature.

　　　　　'I am a man'
　　　　　is not our pure consciousness;
　　　　　it is only our thought!

1466.   That which dwells within all that is,
that through which awareness
itself becomes aware,
that which exists in each thing
as its individual nature,
is the true 'I'
that shines as pure consciousness.

1467.   The indivisible Reality
that dwells within
is consciousness itself.

1468.   The truth of the Self shines as the
pure consciousness underlying the mind.
The fitting course is to discern it in the heart
through being-consciousness
and then to establish it firmly there
through deep contemplation,
so that the fetters of worldly bondage –
the companions of lustful infatuation –
disappear, being revealed as false,
and liberation, the mark of the Real,
shines forth.

1469.   Bitter worldly bondage
          arises through the degrading error
          of mistaking the Self,
          being-consciousness-bliss,
          for the insentient body.

It can only be removed through the certainty of
the experience of Self-inquiry that is filled with
the divine light of consciousness.

1470.   Know that the perfectly pure Self
will well up as a flood of deep peace
in the hearts of those
who have come to know reality as it truly is
through inquiry.

What is required is
to perform worship of that Self
with a collected mind,
so that the mind melts away
through the power of a true love
that is free of guile.

SRI NISARGADATTA MAHARAJ
(1471 – 1530)

1471.　　It is the doing as I tell you
　　　that will bring light, not my telling you.

1472.　　Giving attention to attention, aware
of being aware.　Affectionate awareness is the
crucial factor that brings Reality into focus.

1473.　　Awareness is undivided;
　　　awareness is aware of itself.

1474.　　When this awareness turns upon
　　　itself, you may call it the Supreme State.

1475.　　What you need is
　　　to be aware of being aware.

1476.　　Be aware of being conscious
　　　and seek the source of consciousness.

1477.　　Awareness is unattached and
unshaken.　It is lucid, silent, peaceful, alert and
unafraid, without desire and fear.
Meditate on it as your true being.

1478.   Awareness itself is all important, not the content of it. Deepen and broaden your awareness of yourself and all the blessings will flow.

1479.   You are conscious. Hold on to it.

1480.   The mind must learn that beyond the moving mind there is the background of awareness, which does not change. The mind must come to know the true Self and respect it and cease covering it up.

1481.   The seer becomes conscious
of himself as the seer.

1482.   Mere knowledge is not enough;
the knower must be known.

1483.   To break the spell of the known
the knower must be brought to the forefront.

1484.   Forget the known,
but remember that you are the knower.
Don't be all the time immersed
in your experiences.

1485.   Meet yourself as the knower, apart from the known. Once you know yourself as pure being, the ecstasy of freedom is your own.

1486.   Without the knowledge
of the knower there can be no peace.

1487.   To go beyond you must look away
from the mind and its contents.

1488.   Moods are in the mind
and do not matter. Go within, go beyond.
Cease being fascinated by
the content of your consciousness.

1489.   It is the nature of the mind to roam about. All you can do is to shift the focus of consciousness beyond the mind.

1490.   The all-important word is 'try.'
Allot enough time daily for sitting quietly and trying, just trying to go beyond the personality.

1491.   What matters is the persistence
with which you keep on returning to yourself.

1492.   All you need to do is to try
           and try again.

1493.   You just keep on trying until you succeed. If you persevere, there can be no failure. What matters supremely is sincerity, earnestness; you must really have had surfeit of being the person you are, now see the urgent need of being free of this unnecessary self-identification with a bundle of memories and habits. This steady resistance against the unnecessary is the secret of success.

1494.   Maharaj: It is not a matter of easy, or difficult. You have no alternative.
Either you try or you don't. It is up to you.

Questioner: I have tried many times and failed.
Maharaj: Try again. If you keep on trying, something may happen. But if you don't, you are stuck. You may know all the right words, quote the scriptures, be brilliant in your discussions and yet remain a bag of bones. Or you may be inconspicuous and humble, an insignificant person altogether, yet glowing with loving kindness and deep wisdom.

1495.   The mind will rebel
in the beginning,
but with patience and perseverance
it will yield and keep quiet.

1496.   All our habits go against it
and the task of fighting them
is long and hard sometimes,
but clear understanding helps a lot.

1497.   When I met my Guru, he told me: "You are not what you take yourself to be. Find out what you are. Watch the sense 'I am', find your real Self." I obeyed him, because I trusted him. I did as he told me.

All my spare time I would spend
looking at myself in silence.
And what a difference it made, and how soon!
It took me only three years
to realize my true nature.
My Guru died soon after I met him,
but it made no difference.
I remembered what he told me
and persevered.

1498.   I used to sit for hours together, with nothing but the 'I am' in my mind and soon peace and joy and a deep all-embracing love became my normal state. In it all disappeared – myself, my Guru, the life I lived, the world around me.   Only peace remained and unfathomable silence.

1499.   You have only to look and see.
        Look at your Self, at your own being.

1500.   Awareness is primordial;
it is the original state, beginningless, endless, uncaused, unsupported, without parts, without change.

1501.   All happiness
comes from awareness.   The more we are conscious, the deeper the joy.

1502.   Awareness is the point at which the mind reaches out beyond itself into reality.

1503.   At all times consciousness remains the same. To know it as it is, is realization and timeless peace.

1504.   Do not undervalue attention.
          It means interest and also love.

1505.   Give attention to the reality within
          you and it will come to light.

1506.   Look at yourself, towards yourself,
          into yourself.

1507.   Intelligence is the door to freedom
and alert attention is the mother of intelligence.

1508.   You are in bondage by inadvertence.
          Attention liberates.

1509.   Look at yourself steadily –
          it is enough.

1510.   Seek within.
          Your own Self is your best friend.

1511.   The Self by its nature
          knows itself only.

1512.   Being shines as knowing,
       knowing is warm in love. It is all one.
       You imagine separations
       and trouble yourself with questions.

1513.   Being is consciousness.

1514.   Establish yourself firmly in the awareness of 'I am.' This is the beginning and also the end of all endeavor.

1515.   Why not turn away from the experience to the experiencer and realize the full import of the only true statement you can make: 'I am'?

1516.   Separate the observed from the observer and abandon false identifications.

1517.   Be true to your own Self,
       love your Self absolutely.

1518.   You will be a fully awakened
       witness of the field of consciousness.
       But there should be no feelings and ideas
       to stand between you and the field.

1519.   Maharaj:
How do you go about finding anything?
By keeping your mind and heart on it.
Interest there must be
and steady remembrance.

To remember what needs to be remembered
is the secret of success.

You come to it through earnestness.

Questioner: Do you mean to say that mere
wanting to find out is enough? Surely, both
qualifications and opportunities are needed.

Maharaj: These will come with earnestness.
What is supremely important is to be free from
contradictions: the goal and the way must not
be on different levels; life and light must not
quarrel; behavior must not betray belief.
Call it honesty, integrity, wholeness;
you must not go back, undo, uproot,
abandon the conquered ground.
Tenacity of purpose and honesty in pursuit
will bring you to your goal.

Questioner:

Tenacity and honesty are endowments, surely!
Not a trace of them I have.

> Maharaj: All will come as you go on.
> Take the first step first.
> All blessings come from within.
> Turn within.
> 'I am' you know.
> Be with it all the time you can spare,
> until you revert to it spontaneously.
> There is no simpler and easier way.

1520.   Be interested in yourself
         beyond all experience,
         be with yourself,
         love yourself;
         the ultimate security is found
         only in Self-knowledge.

The main thing is earnestness.

Be honest with yourself.

1521.   Maharaj:
Your own Self is your ultimate teacher.
The outer teacher is merely a milestone.
It is only your inner teacher that will
walk with you to the goal, for he is the goal.

Questioner:
The inner teacher is not easily reached.

Maharaj: Since he is in you and with you,
the difficulty cannot be serious.
Look within, and you will find him.

Questioner: When I look within, I find
sensations and perceptions, thoughts and
feelings, desires and fears, memories and
expectations. I am immersed in this cloud and
see nothing else.

Maharaj: That which sees all this,
and the nothing too, is the inner teacher.
He alone is, all else only appears to be.
He is your own Self,
your hope and assurance of freedom;
find him and cling to him
and you will be saved and safe.

1522.　　It is the person you imagine yourself to be that suffers, not you.　Dissolve it in awareness.　It is merely a bundle of memories and habits.　From the awareness of the unreal to the awareness of your real nature there is a chasm which you will easily cross, once you have mastered the art of pure awareness.

1523.　　Who has not the daring
will not accept the real
even when offered.
Unwillingness born out of fear
is the only obstacle.

1524.　　Only the waking up is important.

1525.　　Meet your own Self.
Be with your own Self,
listen to it, obey it, cherish it,
keep it in mind ceaselessly.
You need no other guide.

1526.　　To become free, your attention must be drawn to the 'I am', the witness.

1527.　　Relax and watch the 'I am.'

1528.   The awareness that you are
will open your eyes to what you are.

It is all very simple.

First of all,
establish a constant contact with your Self,
be with yourself all the time.

Into Self-awareness all blessings flow.

1529.   Evil is the shadow of inattention.
In the light of Self-awareness
it will wither and fall off.

1530.   Only what you discover
through your own awareness,
your own effort,
will be of permanent use to you.

SRI VASISTHA
(1531 - 1569)

1531.   It is by the action of
consciousness becoming aware of itself
that intelligence manifests itself,
not when consciousness apprehends
an inert object.

1532.   The one Self
perceives itself within itself
as the infinite consciousness.

1533.   This ocean of world-appearance
can be crossed only when
you are firmly established in supreme wisdom,
when you see the Self with the Self alone,
and when your intelligence is not diverted
or colored by sense-perceptions.

1534.   Without delay
one should endeavor
to see the Self.

1535.   Contemplate the sole reality of consciousness for the cessation of repeated birth. Taste the pure consciousness, which is, in truth, the very essence of all that exists,
by resolutely renouncing
objectivity of consciousness
(all the concepts and percepts) and contemplating the changeless consciousness which is infinite.

1536.   Know that you are
        the essence of consciousness.

1537.   Remain as pure consciousness
        without any disturbance in it.

1538.   Be firmly established in this wisdom and discard the impure notion of ego-sense from your heart. When the pure heart contemplates the infinite space of consciousness, which is the source of all bliss and which is within easy reach of all,
it rests in the Supreme Self.

1539.   The mind should rest in
pure consciousness as pure consciousness.

1540.   Consciousness alone is the heart of all beings, not the piece of flesh which people call the heart!

1541.   That Self
or the infinite consciousness knows itself by itself; experiences itself in itself by itself.

1542.   Now that you have lost the false characteristic of a mind, you exist as the supreme being or the infinite consciousness, freed from all limitation and conditioning.

1543.   With my vision turned
          upon the Self, I rest in the Self.

1544.   Infinite consciousness,
          which is devoid of concepts
          and extremely subtle, knows itself.

1545.   Consciousness being its own object,
          is consciousness at all times.

1546.   Abandon the habit of apprehending the objects with your mind. The knowers of THAT (Self) have seen what is worth seeing.

1547.   It is the awareness in all that is
     sentient, it knows itself as its own object.

1548.   This is the supreme meditation, this
is the supreme worship: the continuous and
unbroken   awareness   of   the   indwelling
presence, inner light or consciousness.

1549.   One should realize
one's essential nature as pure consciousness.
Thus does one attain liberation.

1550.   The Self realizes the Self,
          the Self sees the Self on account of
          its own Self-luminous nature.

1551.   It is only the Self
          that becomes aware of the Self.

1552.   The consciousness is freed
          from the object.
          There is pure inner consciousness.

1553.   Consciousness becomes conscious
          of its own consciousness;
          it cannot be realized otherwise.

1554.   Only the Self knows the Self.

1555.   Consciousness
         remains consciousness
         and is realized by consciousness.

1556.   Consciousness
         shines as consciousness.

1557.   Since there is neither a contradiction
         nor a division in consciousness
         it is Self-evident.

1558.   Consciousness alone
         exists in consciousness.

1559.   I abandoned all material
         and physical concepts
         and held on to the vision
         of pure consciousness.

1560.   He who is enlightened
         sees not the diversity.

1561.   I practiced concentration.
I sat in the lotus-posture
and remained as pure consciousness.

I gathered all the rays of the mind
which were dissipated over a thousand things
and focused them on my own heart.

1562.   The Self is its own object now
and there is no other externalizing activity.

            Hence,
            it shines in itself as itself.

1563.   The Self knows itself.

1564.   You have heard all this,
            but you do not rest in the truth.

            Only by constant practice
            does this truth become fully established.

1565.   His mind is at rest
who enjoys observing or watching himself
and is disinterested in external events
and observations.

When one's awareness
is thus firmly held within oneself,
the mind abandons its usual restlessness
and flows towards wisdom.

1566.   You are the seer.
          You are consciousness.

1567.   Consciousness
          is conscious of itself
          as consciousness.

1568.   The light of the enlightened itself
          is Self-awareness.

1569.   Behold the light of consciousness
          within your Self by your Self.

SRI SANKARA
(1570 – 1574)

1570.   Turning one's purified awareness within on the witness as pure consciousness, one should gradually bring it to stillness and then become aware of the perfection of one's true nature.

1571.   This has the nature of
Self-awareness, since it is conscious of itself.

1572.   They who rest on the Self that is consciousness, who have put away the outward, the imaginations of the ear and senses, and selfish personality, they verily, are free from the bonds and snares of the world, but not they who only meditate on
what others have seen.

1573.   Through intending
the inner mind to it,
gain the vision of the Self.

1574.   The universal Self
is witness of itself.

CHAPTER TWO

AWARENESS WATCHING AWARENESS

PRACTICE INSTRUCTIONS

PRELIMINARY INSTRUCTIONS
(1-73)

1.   Set aside as much time every day to practice the Awareness Watching Awareness Method as you are willing to set aside.

2.   Every day drop as many unnecessary activities as you can to create more time to practice the Awareness Watching Awareness Method.

3.   If you are not willing to drop all unnecessary activities, in order to create the maximum amount of time every day for practice, then read Chapter (Step) Five in the book *The Seven Steps to Awakening* as many times as needed until the extremely intense desire for Liberation Awakens in you.

Or you could read the book *Inspiration and Encouragement on the Path to Self Realization* (which is the same as Chapter (Step) Five from the book *The Seven Steps to Awakening*) over and over again. If that is not enough you could read the Book *The Desire for Liberation* which is part of the same series. If that is not enough, read one chapter everyday from the book *The Seven Steps to Awakening*. After you finish the book read it again. Read the book *The Seven Steps to Awakening* cover to cover as many times as is necessary to awaken the extremely intense desire for Liberation in you.

4.   Eating food and taking a shower
      are examples of necessary activities.

5.   For some people working to earn a living
      is an example of a necessary activity.

6.   For some people taking care of their
children is an example of a necessary activity.

7.   Some categories of unnecessary activities
      are entertainment, hobbies, etc.

8.   Practice for at least two hours every day. Use all of your free time for practice, and practice for the maximum number of hours per day you are able to.

9.   If you are retired and can practice for twelve hours every day, consider doing so.

10.   It is better if you can be undisturbed and alone during your practice.

11.   If you practice at home, you can ask the people you live with not to disturb you when you are practicing unless there is an emergency.

12.   Or you can find some other place to practice where you will not be disturbed. A quiet place is best.

13.   Bodily posture is not important in the Awareness Watching Awareness Method.

14.   However, since one wishes to turn the attention away from the body, it is important that the body is comfortable and relaxed and not causing any pain.

15.   You can do the practice sitting crossed legged, or sitting on a chair, or sitting on a sofa or couch, or even lying down on your bed if you are able to do so without falling asleep.

16.   Make sure the posture is comfortable and does not cause any pain or strain.

17.   Make sure the posture helps you to ignore the body and turn your attention away from the body.   Make sure the posture does not cause your attention to be directed towards the body.

18.   For the purposes of this practice, the following definitions of the words awareness and thought must be used (19-46):

19.   Thought (19-21): Thoughts are the words of your native language in your mind.

20. If your native language is English, thoughts are those English words in your mind.

21. If you are fluent in two languages, then thoughts are the words of those two languages in your mind.

22. Awareness (22-46): When you wake up from sleep, awareness is that consciousness that woke up from sleep.

23. Thoughts come and thoughts go. The background of awareness does not come and go. The background of awareness is continuous during all your waking hours until you go to sleep again.

24. Awareness is you, your consciousness, just your awareness that is looking through your eyes right now.

25. The words awareness, consciousness, attention, observing, watching, looking, seeing and concentrating all have the same meaning in the practice instructions.

26.   Awareness is not thought.

27.   Awareness is that which is conscious of thought or conscious of the absence of thought.

28.   Both when there are thoughts and when there are no thoughts the background of awareness is aware.

The background of awareness is continuous during all of the waking hours until you go to sleep again.

During deep sleep, the thinker is no longer aware of the background of awareness.

29.   Awareness is not emotions.

30.   Awareness is that which is
        conscious of emotions
        or conscious of the absence of emotions.

31.   Both when there are emotions and when there are no emotions, the background of awareness is aware, because your awareness is continuous during all of the waking hours until you go to sleep again.

32.   Awareness is not the objects
      seen by the eyes.

33.   Awareness is that which is conscious of the objects seen by the eyes or conscious of the absence of the objects seen by the eyes.

34.   Your awareness is aware when the eyes are open seeing objects and when your eyes are closed not seeing objects, because your awareness is continuous during all the waking hours until you go to sleep again.

35.   Awareness is not the thought "I."

36.   Awareness is that which is conscious of the thought "I" or conscious of the absence of the thought "I."

37. Both when you think "I" and when you do not think "I," your awareness is aware, because your awareness is continuous during all the waking hours.

38. Awareness is not desire.

39. Awareness is that which is conscious of desire or conscious of the absence of desire.

40. Both when there is desire and when there is no desire, you are aware, because your awareness is continuous until you go to sleep again.

41. Awareness is not something far away or mysterious.

42. Awareness is that which is looking through your eyes reading this sentence.

43. Just your ordinary, everyday awareness.

44. Not some special awareness.

45.   Awareness is that which wakes up in the morning and remains conscious until you go to sleep at night.

46.   Awareness is not any of the things or experiences perceived.   Awareness is that which is conscious of the things or experiences. Awareness is also that which is conscious of the absence of things or experiences.

47.   Try an experiment (48-52):

48.   Look at an object in the room.

49.   Notice the awareness
looking through your eyes.

50.   Now shut your eyes
and notice that you are still aware.

51.   It is the same awareness
that a moment ago was looking at the room.

52.   Now, with your eyes still closed,
observe your awareness.

53.   The following practice instructions (74-99 or A-Z) are the Awareness Watching Awareness Method described with carefully chosen slightly different words.

54.   The practice instructions
       are called Descriptions.

55.   Use only one Description
       per practice session.

56.   If you are going to practice for one, two or three hours today, then for that entire time, you should use the same Description.

57.   Try Description A first.

58.   Use a different description each day until you have tried all of the Descriptions.

59.   Then choose the Description that was the easiest for you to understand and to practice, and from then on use only that Description.

60.   Some Descriptions might for a moment have you start with your eyes open, however, once you are instructed to close your eyes, keep your eyes closed.

61.   The Awareness Watching Awareness Method is always practiced with the eyes closed.

62.   When you are observing your awareness, just remain with that.

63.   There is no need to do anything else.

64.   Awareness is empty.

65.   It is just awareness being aware of itself.

66.   It is not a special type of awareness.

67.   It is just your ordinary everyday awareness that you normally go through the day with, looking at itself.

68.   You can record the Descriptions on an audiocassette or CD, etc., for your personal use.

69. Record only one Description
     per recording.

70. Listen to only one Description
     during a practice session.

71. It is better not to interrupt your practice
session by having to turn your recording off.

72. That is why it is best to record only
     one Description per recording.

73. Repeat the same Description
     on the recording
     every thirty minutes.

THE

AWARENESS WATCHING AWARENESS

METHOD

PRACTICE INSTRUCTIONS

(74-99 or A-Z):

74.   Description A: Shut your eyes. Notice your awareness. Observe your awareness. Turn your attention away from the world, body and thought and towards awareness watching awareness. Every time you notice you are thinking, turn your attention away from thought and back towards awareness watching awareness. Watch your awareness, not your thoughts.

75.   Description B: Look out at the room and notice your awareness looking out through your eyes. Now shut your eyes and notice the same awareness is still there that a moment ago was looking outward at the room. Observe that awareness. If you notice thoughts, ignore the thoughts and turn your attention away from the thoughts and towards awareness observing awareness.

76.   Description C: Shut your eyes.
Notice that you are conscious.
Watch that consciousness.
Every time you notice a thought,
turn your attention away from the thought
and continue watching your consciousness.
Do not watch your thoughts.
Watch your consciousness.
Consciousness
watching consciousness.
Consciousness conscious of consciousness.

77.   Description D: Shut your eyes.
Turn your attention away from thought
and watch the watcher.

78. Description E: Shut your eyes. Notice your awareness. Be aware of your awareness. If you notice you are thinking, turn your attention away from thought and towards awareness of awareness.

79. Description F: Shut your eyes. Just remain in awareness aware of itself. If there are thoughts, turn your attention away from the thoughts and back to awareness aware of itself.

80. Description G: Shut your eyes. You observe your awareness. Whenever there are thoughts, turn your observation away from the thoughts and continue to observe your awareness.

81. Description H: Shut your eyes. Turn your attention towards awareness and concentrate on awareness. Concentrate in a relaxed manner without effort. Every time thoughts are noticed, turn your attention away from the thoughts and back towards concentrating on awareness.

82.   Description I: Shut your eyes. Be aware of being aware. Now remain in that awareness of awareness. If there are thoughts, turn your awareness away from the thoughts and continue being aware of being aware.

83.   Description J: Shut your eyes. Notice you are aware. Look at that awareness. Remain in awareness looking at awareness. If thoughts arise, look away from the thoughts and continue looking at awareness. Remain in that awareness looking at awareness.

84.   Description K: Shut your eyes.
Your present awareness watching your present awareness, while ignoring all else.

85.   Description L: Look at the room. Notice your attention looking through your eyes. Shut your eyes and turn your attention around to look at itself. Attention attending to attention. Remain with that. Don't move from that. Don't attend to anything else. Don't attend to thought. Attend only to attention.

86.   Description M: Look at the room. Notice your awareness looking through your eyes. Now shut your eyes. Notice that same awareness that was looking through your eyes a moment ago. Now turn that awareness around 180 degrees away from the world, the body and thought and towards itself, towards awareness aware of awareness.

87.   Description N: Look at the room, or if you are outdoors look at the sky. Your awareness is the seer. Shut your eyes. See the seer. Turn your attention away from thought and towards the seer.

88.   Description O: Shut your eyes.
Turn your attention away from the known. Now know the knower.

89.   Description P:

Shut your eyes.
Awareness aware only of awareness.
Remain there. Dwell there. Be there.
Live there.

90. Description Q: Shut your eyes. One awareness observing one awareness. Not two, one observing the other. Only one. Observe your awareness. If you notice thinking, do not attempt to complete the thought. Drop the thought, let go of the thought as though you had no interest in the thought.
Continue observing your awareness.

91. Description R: Shut your eyes. Observe your awareness. Relax into your awareness. Remain there in awareness
aware only of awareness.

92. Description S: Shut your eyes. Turn your awareness away from what your awareness is aware of and towards awareness aware only of itself.

93. Description T: Shut your eyes. Directly experience awareness by observing awareness and relaxing into awareness. Rest in awareness of awareness.
Rest in awareness aware only of itself.
Remain in awareness.
Do not remain in thought.

94.   Description U: There are the things you are aware of. There is the awareness that is aware of the things. Instead of observing the things, observe the awareness. Shut your eyes. There are thoughts and feelings. There is the awareness that is aware of the thoughts and feelings. Instead of observing the thoughts and feelings, observe the awareness.

95.   Description V: Shut your eyes.
Do not observe thought. Observe awareness. Awareness observing awareness is empty. There is no thing to observe there. Don't complicate it by thinking there is more to it. Awareness is subtle. In awareness observing awareness there is only awareness. It is simple. Remain in awareness observing itself.

96. Description W: Shut your eyes. Focus on the awareness that thoughts are arising in. Do not focus on the thoughts. Thoughts come and thoughts go. The awareness in which thoughts are arising does not come and go. Be aware of the awareness that does not come and go. When there are thoughts, watch the awareness, not the thoughts. When there are no thoughts, watch the awareness. Thoughts or no thoughts, continue to observe the awareness. Continue to relax in and be aware of awareness. Remain there. Dwell there.
Be there. Live there.

97. Description X: Shut your eyes. If you see darkness, turn your attention away from the darkness and towards awareness of awareness. If you see light, turn your attention away from the light and towards awareness aware only of awareness. If you notice your breathing, turn your attention away from the breathing and towards awareness aware only of awareness. Whatever you become aware of, turn your attention away from it and towards awareness of awareness.

98.   Description   Y: Shut   your   eyes.
Awareness not aware of thoughts.
Awareness not aware of emotions.
Awareness not aware of anything
except awareness.
Awareness aware of nothing except awareness.
The background of awareness aware only of
the background of awareness.
Awareness aware only of awareness.
Awareness only. Awareness alone.

99.   Description Z: Shut your eyes.
Let go of the idea that you own awareness.
Let go of the idea that you control awareness.
Let the infinite awareness be what it is without
your trying to control it.
Relax and observe the awareness.
Let go of everything
and observe the awareness.
Relax completely and observe the awareness.
With as little effort as possible
and with a gentle, kind, easy, relaxed,
loving approach;
observe the awareness.

CHAPTER THREE

FURTHER CLARIFICATION OF THE

AWARENESS WATCHING AWARENESS

METHOD

1.   These further clarifications have been placed in a separate chapter because the practice instructions for the Awareness Watching Awareness Method are simple and they should remain simple.

2.   It is not helpful
to bring concepts with you into the practice.

3.   It is best just to focus on
the simple practice instructions.

4.   One of the things you might wonder about is what to do after you start watching your awareness.

5.   There is nothing else to be done.

6. You just continue with
awareness watching awareness.

7. There are no objects to see.

8. Awareness is empty.
There is no thing to observe in awareness.

9. Just continue for the entire practice
session watching your awareness.
Only awareness watching awareness
and nothing else.

10. Don't expect any type of experience.

11. If you wonder whether you will have
some kind of spiritual experience, then that
very wondering means you have added
something to awareness watching awareness.

12. Never add anything to
awareness watching awareness.

13. The key is to be content just watching
your awareness and not to move from that
and not to add anything to that.

14. You may or may not have some kind of spiritual experience. However, you should never expect any kind of spiritual experience.

15. If you wonder if the state is going to deepen, that very wondering means you have added something to the Awareness Watching Awareness practice.

16. Never add anything to the
     Awareness Watching Awareness Method.

17. Just be content with
     awareness watching awareness.

18. You should look at it like awareness
     watching awareness is all there is,
     there is nothing more.

19. When practicing the
     Awareness Watching Awareness Method,
     you are not seeking anything.

20. You are observing, not seeking.

21.   If you were seeking something,
      then there would be seeking and
      awareness watching awareness.

22.   That would mean you added seeking to
the awareness watching awareness practice.

23.   Never add anything to the awareness
watching awareness practice. Just be content to
continue with awareness watching awareness
without adding anything to it.

24.   The best practice session is
      when there are no thoughts.

25.   If there are thoughts,
turn your attention away from the thoughts
and towards awareness watching awareness.

26.   Do not encourage thoughts.

27.   Do not try to complete a thought.

28.   Do not turn your attention
      towards thoughts.

29.   Do not think about thinking.

30.   If thoughts are happening, do not make a problem out of it.   Just turn your attention away from thoughts and towards awareness watching awareness.

31.   Just remain with
      awareness watching awareness.

32.   When awareness is watching awareness
      something extraordinary is happening.

33.   You are for the first time turning inward.

34.   Your true nature is awareness.

35.   What you really are at your core
      is awareness.

36.   Therefore,
      in awareness watching awareness,
      you are for the first time
      observing and knowing yourself.

37.   However, you should not think about that or anything else written in this chapter while practicing awareness watching awareness, because then you would be adding those thoughts to the practice.

38.   The reason for pointing out that you are doing something extraordinary while practicing awareness watching awareness is because at first you might think, "what else?" or "so what?"

39.   Just continue to practice and forget about "what else?" or "so what?"

40.   By turning your attention away from thoughts and towards awareness watching awareness, you are doing something that will change your life completely, if you are sincere and continue to practice.

41.   Most humans live their entire lives
       always looking outward
       at people, places and things.

42. By turning your attention away from the world, body and thought and towards awareness watching awareness, you are doing something extraordinary.

43. It might take a few days, a few weeks, or for some people a few months to start to feel something.

44. At first it is subtle and you won't know what it is. You will know that you like it.

45. It is pleasant.

46. A new subtle feeling.

47. You are beginning to feel: eternal-life-love-peace.

48. However, you should not have any expectations about that, because if you expect that, then you are adding that expectation to your awareness watching awareness practice.

49. Never add anything to your awareness watching awareness practice.

50. Just remain in awareness watching awareness while ignoring all else.

51. Just stay there.

52. Just remain in that.

53. Don't look for something else.

54. While you are practicing the Awareness Watching Awareness Method (55-89):

55. Just stay there.

56. Relax there.

57. Don't seek something
other than awareness watching awareness.

58. Don't seek any other state.

59. Don't seek deeper awareness.

60. Don't seek anything.

61.   Just remain in
      awareness watching awareness.

62.   Be happy that it is simple.

63.   Don't seek more than that.

64.   It is just a simple state.

65.   Don't seek peace.

66.   Let peace come on its own, if it is going to
come, without your expecting or seeking it.

67.   Just remain with awareness watching
awareness, and every time a thought arises
turn your awareness away from the thought
and towards awareness watching awareness.

68.   Continue to practice every day.

69.   Look at it as though all you were seeking
was the awareness watching awareness itself
and not something else.
Be content with staying in awareness watching
awareness without moving from it.

70. Some days the mind may be noisy, however, if you keep on practicing, a good day will appear when your practice will go very deep without your trying to make it go deep.

71. Never think about deep or shallow.

72. If you think about deep or shallow,
you would be adding something to
the awareness watching awareness practice.

73. Just be content to remain with awareness watching awareness, regardless if it seems like a good practice session or not.

74. Some days
your emotions may be turbulent.

75. Ignore the turbulent feelings and turn your attention away from the emotions and towards awareness watching awareness.

76. If you continue practicing the
Awareness Watching Awareness Method
every day, eventually you will start to enjoy awareness watching awareness.

77.   How long it will take to begin enjoying
       awareness watching awareness
       is different for different people.

78.   It may take days, weeks
       or for some people months
       before they begin to enjoy the practice.

79.   The point is, if you find it difficult to
remain with awareness watching awareness in
the beginning, don't give up. Practice every
day on the good days and on the noisy-mind or
turbulent-feeling days also.

80.   Just continue turning your attention
       away from thoughts and towards
       awareness watching awareness.

81.   You should not be expecting the day
when you will start to enjoy
awareness watching awareness,
because then you would be adding something
to the awareness watching awareness practice.

82.   The best kind of awareness watching
awareness practice session is one that is empty.

83. Awareness watching awareness
    and nothing else.

84. Just stay there.

85. Just be there.

86. Dwell there.

87. Remain there.

88. Don't seek anything different; just be
content with awareness watching awareness.

89. Relax and continue
    watching your awareness.

90. Here is a way to look at it (91-103):

91. Awareness watching awareness
    is similar to falling in love.

92. You spend time with someone.

93. You watch them. You observe them.

94. You do not yet know them.

95. You continue to observe them.

96. You don't have expectations,
because you don't know them well enough yet
to have expectations.

97. You continue to observe them.

98. Some days you have pleasant feelings
     while you observe them.

99. Some days you have unpleasant feelings
     while you observe them.

100. You continue to observe them.

101. Every day you come to know them better,
      even though you may not be aware that
      you are coming to know them better.

102. Then one day,
      suddenly and unexpectedly,
      you fall in Love.

103. Awareness watching awareness
    is similar to that.

104. Just don't expect anything,
    and continue watching your awareness.

105. The fact that nothing is happening
    is great!

106. If it seems like day after day it is just the
same, only awareness watching awareness;
that is great!

107. Just remain content with that.

108. If you think it is going to change,
then you are adding something to
awareness watching awareness, in the form of
an expectation that it is going to change.

109. Look at awareness watching awareness
    as enough, just as it is.

110. Continue your practice every day.

111. When will you fall in Love with
     awareness watching awareness?

112. It may be after one month
     or after many months or years of practice.

113. There may or may not be
     confirmation along the way.

114. Do not be concerned about whether you
are progressing or not. Progress may be
imperceptible to the practitioner.

115. Some people will reach the point where
just closing their eyes brings awareness-joy
even before they have started the practice.

116. You should not expect it,
because then you have added something to the
Awareness Watching Awareness Method.

117. Some people may experience turbulence
     for many years before peace or vice versa.

118. Persevere and continue to practice.

119. You can look upon your awareness as something that wants you to watch it without expecting anything from it, like someone who wants to be loved for what they are and not for what they can give you.

120. Continue to watch awareness
and do not expect peace-love-joy.

121. Let peace-love-joy come on its own,
without your expecting it.

122. What you truly are is Absolutely Perfect Infinite-Eternal-Awareness-Love-Bliss.

123. By having your attention turned towards the world, the body and thought all the time, you imagine you are a body subject to disease, death and suffering.

124. By turning your attention
towards awareness,
you are for the first time
observing what you are.

125. When practicing
do not think about what you are.

126. Watch awareness
without expecting anything.

127. Don't watch your thoughts.

128. Turn your attention away from your
thoughts and watch your empty awareness.

129. Observe the observing.

130. Observe the awareness.

131. If you remain content with
awareness watching awareness,
your problems will start to disappear.

132. Your misery will start to disappear.

133. Peace will come unexpectedly.

134. Joy will come unexpectedly.

135. Infinite Love will come unexpectedly.

136. Awareness watching awareness is awareness being awareness.

137. Because of the long ancient habit of looking outward towards people, places and things, the word "watching" is used in some of the practice instructions.

138. One takes that same habit of watching people, places and things and shuts the eyes and turns it inwards towards awareness watching awareness.

139. That is why the word "watching" is used in some of the practice instructions.

140. What is real is awareness watching awareness, looking inward.

141. What is unreal is looking outward towards the world of people, places and things.

142. Looking outward brings suffering, death and futility.

143. Watching thoughts is not looking inward.

144. Watching feelings is not looking inward.

145. Watching breathing
is not looking inward.

146. Only turning the attention away from
the observed and towards the observer
is looking inward.

147. Only awareness watching awareness
is looking inward.

148. Looking inward is eternal liberation.

149. Looking inward is eternal life.

150. Looking inward is eternal awareness.

151. Looking inward is eternal peace.

152. Looking inward is eternal joy.

153. Looking inward is eternal Love
that is absolutely perfect
and free of all forms
of sorrow and misery.

154. That joy, that perfection,
     is your awareness.

155. Because you always looked outward,
     you never experienced it.

156. To change the long habit of looking
     outward, you need to practice every day.

157. Practice for as many hours every day
     as you can.

158. If you only practice the
Awareness Watching Awareness Method
for thirty minutes per day and spend the other
twenty-three and a half hours looking outward,
you will not progress very quickly.

159. If you want rapid results,
drop all your unnecessary activities
to create the maximum amount of time
to practice for many hours every day.

160. Maybe once per week,
you can devote the whole day to practicing
awareness watching awareness.

161. To come to know, experience, and live in
Infinite-Eternal-Awareness-Love-Bliss
is definitely worth the time spent practicing.

162. You will discover
you are not a body living in a world.

163. You are eternal awareness,
perfect love-joy.

164. Don't expect any of the experiences
described in this chapter,
expectation will destroy the effectiveness.

165. If it seems boring
the first few times you try
the awareness watching awareness practice
that is okay.

Continue to practice.

The eternal end of all sorrow and suffering
and the eternal experience of
Absolutely Perfect
Infinite-Awareness-Love-Bliss
is worth all of the time devoted to practice.

Please use the contact form at seeseer.com to let us know if reading the book Self Awareness Practice Instructions was helpful.

The six books in the Self Realization series are:

1.   Self Awareness Practice Instructions.

The most direct and rapid means to Self Realization goes by various names including:

A.   Self Inquiry.
B.   Self Abidance.
C.   Self Attention.
D.   Self Awareness.
E.   Abiding as Awareness.
F.   Awareness of Awareness.
G.   Awareness Aware of Itself.
H.   Awareness Watching Awareness.

The book Self Awareness Practice Instructions contains all of the quotes in Chapter (Step) Seven from the book The Seven Steps to Awakening and also both Chapter Seven: Practice Instructions for the Awareness Watching Awareness Method and Chapter Eight: Further Clarification of the Awareness Watching Awareness Method from the book The Most Direct Means to Eternal Bliss.

2.   The Desire for Liberation.

The awakening of the extremely intense desire for Liberation is the most important aid to Self Realization. The book The Desire for Liberation contains all of the quotes in Chapter (Step) Four from the book The Seven Steps to Awakening and both Chapter Four: The Desire for Liberation and Chapter Five: How to Awaken the Extremely Intense Desire for Liberation from the book The Most Direct Means to Eternal Bliss.

3.   *The False self.*

The false self goes by many different names including:

A.   *Ego.*
B.   *Mind.*
C.   *Thinking*
D.   *A bundle of thoughts*
E.   *The impostor self.*

The book The False self contains all of the quotes in Chapter (Step) Three from the book The Seven Steps to Awakening. It also contains the contents of Chapter One: The Impostor, Chapter Two: The Impostor's Tricks and Chapter Three: The Impostor's Tools from the book The Most Direct Means to Eternal Bliss.

4.   *Inspiration and Encouragement*
        on the Path to Self Realization.

This collection of quotes is for the purpose of inspiring, encouraging and motivating those who are seeking Self Realization.

That includes being inspired, encouraged and motivated to:

A. Make and maintain the decision to bring the impostor self to its final end and thus to remain eternally as your true Self which is Absolutely Perfect Infinite-Awareness-Love-Bliss that has never experienced any sorrow or suffering in all of eternity.

B. Drop all of your unnecessary activities and use all of the free time thus created to practice the most direct and rapid means leading to Self Realization. The Seven Sages placed tremendous emphasis on the importance of practice.

The more times you read these quotes the better. Read all of these quotes every day, or at least be sure to read them every time you feel the need to be inspired, encouraged or motivated to get back on track in one-pointedness towards your spiritual goal and spiritual practice. The quotes in this book are the same as the quotes in Chapter (Step) Five from the book The Seven Steps to Awakening.

5.   Everything is an Illusion.

What is helpful about reading these types of quotes is that the more you can realize that everything is an illusion the better you can ignore everything and turn inward. One of the most significant aspects to this collection of quotes by the Seven Sages is that in addition to pointing out that everything is a dreamlike illusion, they also point out in many of their quotes that upon Self Realization everything disappears. This book contains all of the quotes in Chapter (Step) Two from the book The Seven Steps to Awakening.

6.   How Not to Get Lost in Concepts.

A mistake made by almost everyone who studies the Direct Path teachings is that instead of using the teachings as practice instructions they become lost in spiritual concepts. Most of those people never correct that mistake and at the end of their physical life they are still lost in a maze of concepts without having realized the Self. This book contains all of the quotes in Chapter (Step) One from the book The Seven Steps to Awakening.

For more information about these books go to:

www.seeseer.com

CPSIA information can be obtained at www.ICGtesting.com
Printed in the USA
LVOW11s0435140314

377242LV00002B/508/P